EPIGRAPH

In every new dawn, in every drop of water, in every leaf that sways in the wind, lies a strong call to our conscience: to take care of this planet is to take care of ourselves today and an essential legacy for the living beings of the future.

This book is dedicated to all those who in their daily actions decide to be guardians of the Earth, who dare to dream and work for a world where green is not only a beautiful color, but the symbol of a sustainable future.

THE AUTHOR

THE AGE OF GREEN MAINTENANCE: TRANSFORMING COMMERCE, SERVICES AND INDUSTRY, PRESERVING THE PLANET

PREFACE

In a world marked by unmistakable signs of environmental alarm, the transition to sustainable maintenance practices has been transformed from a desirable option to an imperative necessity.

This book, entirely dedicated to the concept of Green Maintenance, was born as a direct response to the urgent need to safeguard our planet to ensure its future prosperity.

We are at a critical point, where the climate crisis and environmental degradation challenge us to seek solutions that not only mitigate our negative impact, but also promote a regenerative and harmonious coexistence with the natural environment.

Green Maintenance thus stands as a beacon of hope, offering a viable path to sustainability.

The adoption of sustainable maintenance practices reveals its benefits in three interconnected spheres: environmental, economic and social. From an environmental perspective, by minimizing our ecological footprint and conserving natural resources, we actively contribute to the protection of biodiversity and climate stability, ensuring a vital environment for the diversity of life on our planet.

From the economic angle, Green Maintenance opens doors to efficiency and innovation. Optimizing the use of energy and materials not only enables companies to reduce their operating costs and strengthen their competitiveness, but also catalyzes opportunities for sustainable growth.

This approach to sustainability translates into increased appeal to environmentally conscious consumers and employees, enhancing corporate reputation and strengthening ties with the community.

Perhaps the most significant aspect of sustainable maintenance, however, is its impact on society. By adopting practices that protect the environment and promote social equity, we are laying the foundation for healthier, more resilient and inclusive communities.

From improving air quality to creating sustainable job opportunities and promoting comprehensive environmental justice, Green Maintenance is positioned as an essential pillar for a flourishing and equitable future.

Throughout this book, we will delve into the fundamental principles of sustainable maintenance, from its definition and scope to its implementation in the real world.

Through inspiring stories, practical tools and effective strategies, we will provide our readers with the resources they need to turn their maintenance operations into true agents of positive change.

In the hope that this book will serve as both a guide and an inspiration to those committed to the legacy of a greener, more sustainable future, I invite you to join this transformative journey.

Together, we can chart a course toward a restored balance between humanity and nature, thus ensuring a legacy of well-being and prosperity for generations to come.

INTRODUCTION

In the vast array of global challenges we face today, sustainable development and environmental conservation emerge not only as desirable objectives, but as categorical imperatives to ensure the well-being of our planet and future generations.

Within this context, the concept of Green Maintenance reveals itself as an essential backbone for building a more prosperous, just and equitable future.

This book arises in response to the urgent need to redefine our maintenance practices, guiding us towards the adoption of an ethic of care and regeneration of our natural environment.

THE EVOLUTION OF GREEN MAINTENANCE

Green Maintenance is an operating philosophy and a set of practices that seek to minimize the negative environmental impact associated with the maintenance of infrastructure, machines and systems, while promoting efficiency and conservation of natural resources.

This approach goes far beyond mere repair or routine maintenance. It is a holistic perspective that integrates sustainability principles into all stages of the asset life cycle, from design and use to eventual decommissioning or refurbishment.

THE IMPERATIVE NEED FOR GREEN MAINTENANCE TODAY

The planet is sending us increasingly clear and alarming signals: climate change is accelerating its devastating effects, species are becoming extinct at an unprecedented rate, and air and water pollution are compromising the health of millions of people.

Faced with this reality, Green Maintenance is a critical and necessary response. It is not only a question of environmental responsibility; it is a vital strategy for preserving the planet's biodiversity, ensuring the availability of natural resources and promoting a healthy environment for all.

HOW THIS BOOK DRIVES THE TRANSFORMATION TO SUSTAINABILITY

Aimed at a broad audience ranging from directors, managers, administrators, supervisors and maintenance professionals to individuals conscious of their environmental impact, this book is intended to be a comprehensive and practical guide to incorporating Green Maintenance into the core of day-to-day operations.

Through an enriching mix of relevant theory, applied examples and effective strategies, readers will gain the indispensable tools to adopt and execute Green Maintenance in a variety of operational contexts.

From the careful evaluation of existing practices to the meticulous implementation of sustainable programs, the book offers a clear perspective and a detailed path to innovation in sustainability.

It focuses on inspiring readers to be proactive agents of change, equipping them with the knowledge and skills necessary to lead the transition to maintenance practices that not only respect, but also regenerate our environment.

A COMMITMENT TO THE FUTURE

Green Maintenance transcends the idea of being a simple alternative; it is a call to deeply rethink how we interact with the world around us. This book is offered as a key piece on the road to a reality where sustainable maintenance is not the exception, but the rule.

It invites us to reflect on the legacy we wish to leave for future generations. Through its pages, we embark on a journey of transformation, not only as maintenance professionals and practitioners, but as members of a global community united by the common goal of preserving the vitality of our planet.

By embracing the principles and practices of Green Maintenance, we take a crucial step towards building a more sustainable, just and prosperous future.

This book is not just a guide; it is a catalyst for change, inviting us all to be part of the solution.

REFLECTION ON THE CURRENT ENVIRONMENTAL SITUATION

At the dawn of the 21st century, we are at a critical turning point in our relationship with planet Earth. The environmental warning signs have become not only more evident, but also more alarming.

Climate change is advancing with relentless speed, manifesting itself in extreme events ranging from unprecedented heat waves to devastating hurricanes, raging wildfires and massive losses of biodiversity.

The accumulation of plastics in our oceans, air pollution in our cities and the degradation of our soils and freshwater sources are just some of the symptoms of an environmental crisis that threatens the sustainability of life as we know it.

This situation, far from being an isolated phenomenon, is the cumulative result of decades of unsustainable practices in almost every aspect of human activity, from agriculture and industry to the very core of our economies and lifestyles.

In this context, the concept of green maintenance emerges not only as a desirable innovation, but also as an imperative need.

Green maintenance represents a unique opportunity to reverse some of the damage done and lay the groundwork for a more sustainable future. This approach focuses on adopting practices that reduce the negative environmental impact of infrastructure and equipment maintenance operations, while promoting efficiency, resource conservation and greater harmony with the natural environment.

Through this lens, maintenance ceases to be a mere operational task and becomes a comprehensive sustainability strategy.

THE CRUCIAL ROLE OF GREEN MAINTENANCE

Green maintenance acts as a catalyst for sustainability by incorporating environmentally responsible practices into the daily maintenance and operations routine.

For example, the use of environmentally friendly materials and products, the optimization of energy and resource consumption, and the implementation of efficient waste management systems are measures that contribute significantly to reducing the ecological footprint of any organization.

In addition, green maintenance is closely aligned with the principles of the circular economy, seeking not only efficiency in the use of resources, but also the reuse, recycling and regeneration of materials and energy.

This holistic approach not only addresses the symptoms of the environmental crisis, but also focuses on its underlying causes, promoting a fundamental change in the way we conceive and carry out the maintenance of our infrastructures and equipment.

CHAPTER 1: FUNDAMENTALS OF GREEN MAINTENANCE

DEFINITION OF GREEN MAINTENANCE

Green Maintenance, in its essence, represents a conscious and proactive strategy towards the conservation and optimization of resources in the management of assets and infrastructures.

By adopting a sustainability-first approach, it seeks not only to reduce the ecological footprint associated with the operation and maintenance of these assets, but also to promote a culture of responsibility and respect for the environment among its stakeholders.

A distinctive feature of Green Maintenance is its commitment to innovation and the adoption of clean technologies and energy efficiency practices. This includes the implementation of renewable energy systems, optimization of water use, reduction of harmful emissions and efficient waste management.

The application of these practices not only contributes to the preservation of the environment, but can also result in significant savings over time, demonstrating that sustainability and economic viability can go hand in hand.

In addition, Green Maintenance encourages the participation and education of everyone involved, from operators and technicians, to end users and the community at large.

This inclusion seeks to create a collective awareness of the importance of sustainable practices and how each individual action can contribute to a greater positive impact.

On a practical level, Green Maintenance is materialized through the adoption of environmental standards and certifications that guide maintenance operations and practices. These frameworks not only establish clear and measurable criteria for sustainability, but also offer recognition and added value to entities that demonstrate a genuine commitment to the environment.

Finally, Green Maintenance looks to the future, anticipating and adapting to changes in environmental regulations, societal expectations and technological innovations. This dynamic approach ensures that maintenance practices are not only sustainable today, but also remain relevant and effective in the future, guaranteeing a legacy of sustainability for generations to come.

In short, Green Maintenance is a comprehensive philosophy that encapsulates responsibility, efficiency and innovation in asset and infrastructure management, projecting a path towards a more sustainable future that respects our planet.

HISTORY AND EVOLUTION OF GREEN MAINTENANCE

The history and evolution of Green Maintenance is intertwined with the development of the global environmental movement, marking a fundamental shift in how societies and companies approach the management of their environmental resources and impacts.

This concept, although rooted in the ideals of the 1970s and 1980s, is rooted in the early realization that human practices cannot continue without considering their effect on the planet.

In its early days, Green Maintenance focused on relatively simple and straightforward practices, such as improving the energy efficiency of machinery and reducing waste generation in industrial processes.

However, what began as isolated and specific measures, over time, evolved into a broader and more structured movement.

The energy crises of the 1970s, along with the growing visibility of environmental problems such as acid rain, air and water pollution, and ozone depletion, acted as catalysts, prompting both individuals and organizations to reconsider and reformulate their practices toward more sustainable models.

As we moved toward the end of the 20th century and into the new millennium, globalization and technological advances led to greater global awareness and connectivity.

Environmental challenges, such as climate change and biodiversity loss, have become prevalent topics of discussion, not only within the scientific and environmental communities, but also in political, economic and social forums worldwide.

This increased visibility fostered a rapid evolution of Green Maintenance from a niche focus to a strategic priority for companies and governments.

The new millennium brought with it a deeper and more nuanced understanding of sustainability, seeing Green Maintenance not only in terms of mitigating negative impacts, but also as an opportunity to create economic, social and environmental value in an integrated manner. The adoption of clean technologies, circular economy practices, and the integration of sustainability criteria in strategic decision making became fundamental pillars. Certification in environmental standards such as ISO 14001 and LEED, for example, began to be seen as a competitive differentiator in the market.

Today, Green Maintenance is understood as a critical component of Corporate Social Responsibility (CSR) and corporate sustainability, reflecting a profound shift in corporate and governmental mindsets.

This approach encompasses a wide range of practices, from sustainable design and energy efficiency to biodiversity and social inclusion, representing an evolution from the reactive strategies of the past to a proactive and holistic view of maintenance.

Looking to the future, Green Maintenance will continue to evolve in response to new challenges and opportunities. Technological innovation, cross-sector collaboration and a commitment to education and community involvement will play crucial roles in shaping this future, ensuring that Green Maintenance remains at the forefront of the global quest for sustainability.

In this dynamic context, the Green Maintenance story is not only a testament to our collective journey towards greater respect for our planet, but also a map towards a more sustainable and resilient future.

INFLUENCES AND CONVERGENCE OF MOVEMENTS

The trajectory of green maintenance not only reflects a growing concern for the environmental impact of human activities, but also highlights how the convergence of movements, regulations and legislation has shaped its development and adoption.

This multifaceted influence has created an interconnected web of efforts that collectively seek to mitigate the effects of climate change and promote a more sustainable future.

Since its inception, green maintenance has been closely linked to the global environmental movement, which has played a crucial role in raising awareness of issues such as global warming, deforestation, pollution and biodiversity loss.

These movements have served not only to educate the public and corporations about the importance of sustainable practices, but also to pressure governments to take concrete action. The result has been a series of stricter environmental legislation and regulations that set minimum standards for resource conservation and pollution reduction.

In parallel, there has been a notable influence of international agreements and protocols on climate change, such as the Kyoto Protocol and the Paris Agreement, which have encouraged countries to commit to greenhouse gas emission reduction targets.

These agreements have catalyzed the development of national policies and sustainability initiatives, establishing a framework for the implementation of green maintenance practices in various sectors.

In addition, the concept of circular economy has gained ground, promoting a product life cycle that minimizes waste and makes the best use of resources. This idea has strongly influenced green maintenance, emphasizing the need to consider sustainable design, reuse, recycling and end-of-life product recovery.

This approach has led to greater integration of practices, which not only seek to reduce environmental impact, but also to improve the economic efficiency and resilience of supply chains.

The adoption of green and renewable technologies has been another critical factor, driven by technological advances, government incentives and market demand.

The integration of renewable energy, electric vehicles, green buildings and environmental management systems into maintenance operations reflects how the convergence of technological innovation and the demand for sustainable solutions is reshaping business and government practices.

Finally, the growing demand for transparency and accountability on the part of consumers and shareholders has encouraged greater adoption of green housekeeping practices.

The preference for sustainable products and services, coupled with scrutiny of corporate practices, has pushed companies to incorporate sustainability into their strategic core, seeing it not only as an ethical and legal obligation, but also as a competitive advantage.

DIFFERENTIATION FROM TRADITIONAL MAINTENANCE

The differentiation between traditional maintenance and the more contemporary approach of green maintenance is key to understanding how asset and infrastructure management practices have evolved in response to environmental and sustainability imperatives.

While traditional maintenance has historically focused on maximizing operational efficiency and minimizing operating and maintenance costs, it has often done so without thorough consideration of the environmental implications of such practices.

This approach has proven to be effective in terms of maintaining the operability and reliability of assets in the short term, but can have negative consequences in terms of resource use and waste generation, leading to adverse environmental impact in the long term.

Traditional maintenance, characteristically reactive, tends to focus on repairing equipment and systems only after they have failed or shown signs of deterioration.

This method, which can reduce initial operating costs, often results in higher total expenditure and more intensive use of resources due to unplanned emergency repairs, equipment replacements and unscheduled shutdowns.

In addition, disregard for resource efficiency and waste management can lead to practices that, while economically viable in the short term, are unsustainable from an environmental perspective.

On the other hand, green maintenance takes a proactive and holistic approach, considering the entire life cycle of assets and their environmental impact, from acquisition and use to final disposal.

This approach focuses not only on maintaining the functionality and efficiency of the assets, but also on minimizing their environmental footprint by reducing energy consumption, optimizing the use of resources, reducing emissions and properly managing waste.

Green maintenance also promotes the adoption of clean technologies and maintenance practices that are energy efficient and less harmful to the environment.

The adoption of predictive maintenance strategies, which use real-time monitoring technologies and data analysis to anticipate failures before they occur, is another important distinction of green maintenance compared to the traditional approach. This type of maintenance not only helps prevent unexpected outages and extend equipment life, but also contributes to a more efficient and less wasteful operation.

In addition, while traditional maintenance may not consider the impact of decommissioning and disposal practices, green maintenance emphasizes the importance of recycling and reusing components and materials at the end of the assets' useful life, promoting a circular economy and reducing the demand for new resources.

KEY DIFFERENTIATING ASPECTS

The key differentiators between traditional maintenance and green maintenance highlight an evolution towards more conscious and sustainable practices in asset and infrastructure management.

These differences are reflected not only in the technical and operational implementation, but also in the underlying philosophy and long-term objectives of maintenance strategies.

Green maintenance prioritizes the use of materials and technologies that have a low environmental impact throughout their life cycle. This means preferring recyclable, biodegradable or sustainably sourced materials and the use of technologies that are energy efficient and reduce greenhouse gas emissions.

Careful selection of these materials and technologies not only reduces the ecological footprint of maintenance operations, but can also improve efficiency and reduce long-term operating costs, in contrast to the traditional approach, which often privileges availability and upfront cost over sustainability.

Green maintenance implements work practices designed to minimize material waste and unnecessary energy consumption. This may include repair techniques that extend component life, the use of high-efficiency tools and machinery, and operating procedures that reduce the amount of waste generated.

Unlike traditional maintenance, which may not focus on these aspects, green maintenance seeks to optimize each process to operate as efficiently and sustainably as possible.

Another key differentiator of green maintenance is its focus on end-of-life sustainability. Rather than simply discarding equipment and materials, green maintenance looks for ways to recycle, reuse or renew resources at the end of their use cycle.

This may include programs to return obsolete equipment to the manufacturer for recycling, the sale of used components for reuse, or the donation of recyclable materials to communities, educational centers, associations or projects that can benefit from them.

This approach contrasts sharply with traditional practices, where waste at the end of an asset's useful life is often not managed sustainably.

Green maintenance is also distinguished by a continuous commitment to improvement and innovation. By constantly searching for new ways to reduce the environmental impact of maintenance practices, this approach encourages experimentation and the adoption of emerging technologies.

This can range from using artificial intelligence to optimize operations to experimenting with new biodegradable materials. In contrast, traditional maintenance can be more resistant to change, prioritizing established and proven practices.

Finally, green maintenance implies an integration of sustainability into the organizational culture, where all decisions are made considering their environmental impact. This requires ongoing education and training for employees, as well as policies and procedures that reflect these values.

Unlike the more narrow focus of traditional maintenance, green maintenance sees sustainability as a core value and an integral part of the organization's mission and vision.

BENEFITS AND CHALLENGES OF TRANSITION

The transition to green maintenance, despite its clear benefits, is not without its challenges. This path towards more sustainable practices in asset and infrastructure management promises not only improved efficiency and environmental sustainability, but also significant economic and strategic advantages.

However, achieving these benefits requires overcoming certain obstacles inherent to the change process.

Long-Term Operating Cost Reductions: One of the most tangible benefits of green maintenance is the reduction of operating costs over time. Through optimization of resource use, energy efficiency and waste reduction, organizations can experience a decrease in energy, materials and waste management expenses.

In addition, predictive and proactive maintenance can reduce unplanned outages and extend equipment life, resulting in significant savings.

Improved Corporate Reputation: In an increasingly environmentally conscious marketplace, adopting green maintenance practices can substantially improve a company's public perception. This not only attracts customers who value sustainability, but can also be a determining factor in attracting and retaining talent, as well as opening up new business opportunities in sustainability-oriented sectors.

Compliance with Environmental Regulations: As environmental regulations become more stringent globally, the transition to green maintenance ensures compliance with these regulations, avoiding fines and penalties. In addition, exceeding minimum standards can offer companies competitive advantages, such as access to tax incentives and markets that highly value green credentials.

Need for Upfront Investments: Implementing green maintenance practices can require significant investments in technology, staff training and process re-engineering. These initial costs can be an obstacle, especially for small and medium-sized companies with limited budgets. However, it is important to note that these investments are usually recouped in the medium to long term, through the savings generated.

Resistance to Change Within Organizations: Changing established practices and organizational culture, can be met with internal resistance, both from leadership and management, as well as from employees. Overcoming this challenge requires strong leadership, effective communication and training programs that emphasize the personal and collective benefits of sustainable practices.

Adapting to Emerging Technologies: The rapid pace of technological innovation can be both an opportunity and a challenge. Keeping up with the latest green maintenance tools and techniques requires a continuous commitment to learning and adapting, which can be overwhelming for some organizations.

Measuring and Communicating Impacts: Demonstrating the tangible benefits of green maintenance can be complicated, especially when it comes to measuring return on investment (ROI) and environmental impacts. Developing and applying effective metrics is crucial, to communicate success and justify the transition to more sustainable practices.

The transition to green maintenance offers numerous benefits, including reductions in long-term operating costs, improved corporate reputation and compliance with environmental regulations. However, it faces challenges such as the need for upfront investments and resistance to change within organizations.

IMPORTANCE IN THE ERA OF SUSTAINABILITY

In the current context, marked by growing environmental awareness and a global call to action in the face of climate change, the importance of green maintenance in the era of sustainability cannot be underestimated.

This approach, focused on environmentally friendly maintenance practices, is closely aligned with the broader concept of corporate sustainability, which seeks to harmonize economic objectives with the principles of social and environmental responsibility.

As we move towards a more sustainable future, green maintenance emerges as a critical tool for organizations wishing to thrive in this new paradigm.

Ecological Footprint Reduction: Green maintenance plays a key role in minimizing the environmental impact of corporate operations. Through optimization of resource use, energy efficiency, and proper waste management, organizations can significantly reduce their ecological footprint.

This not only contributes to environmental protection, but also responds to the expectations of consumers, investors and regulators, who are demanding more sustainable business practices.

Strengthening Market Competitiveness: In an environment where sustainability has become a key differentiator, green maintenance practices can improve an organization's competitive position.

Companies that demonstrate a genuine commitment to sustainability often enjoy an enhanced reputation, which can translate into greater customer loyalty, competitive advantage and ultimately improved financial performance.

Meeting Stakeholder Expectations: The adoption of green maintenance practices is also critical to meeting the growing demands of stakeholders, who now expect companies to act as responsible corporate citizens.

This includes not only complying with stricter environmental regulations, but also proactively adopting practices that go beyond what is legally required, demonstrating a genuine commitment to sustainability.

Despite its growing importance, implementing green maintenance strategies is not without its challenges. It requires upfront investments, staff training and often a re-evaluation of existing processes and practices.

However, these initial investments are offset in the long term by the economic, environmental and social benefits they bring.

In addition, the integration of innovative technologies such as the Internet of Things Application (IoTA) and Artificial Intelligence (AI) offer new opportunities to further optimize maintenance practices and strengthen sustainability efforts.

Looking ahead, it is clear that green maintenance will play an increasingly crucial role in corporate strategy. As companies seek to align with the United Nations Sustainable Development Goals and respond to regulatory and market pressures, maintenance practices that prioritize sustainability will become the norm, not the exception.

In addition, as technology continues to advance, new opportunities will arise to improve efficiency and further reduce the environmental impact of corporate operations.

FUTURE PROSPECTS

The future horizon of green maintenance looks not only promising but also essential on the road to greater global sustainability.

The integration of technological advances such as the Internet of Things Application (IoTA), artificial intelligence (AI) and the principles of the circular economy is profoundly transforming maintenance strategies and practices, projecting a future in which operational efficiency and environmental responsibility converge in an unprecedented way.

IoTA is revolutionizing green maintenance by offering unprecedented connectivity between devices and sensors. This interconnectivity facilitates real-time data collection and analysis, enabling predictive maintenance that can anticipate failures before they occur, minimizing resource waste and extending equipment life.

In the future, we expect to see an even greater expansion of IoTA in green maintenance, with more sophisticated sensor networks and intelligent devices, capable of self-diagnosis and self-adjustment, optimizing their own efficiency and reducing their environmental impact.

AI is set to play a crucial role in green maintenance, providing the ability to analyze vast amounts of data from IoTA to identify patterns, predict trends and suggest optimal maintenance actions.

This technology can significantly improve decision making, enabling more accurate and timely interventions that save energy and resources. In addition, AI can facilitate the design of more efficient systems and processes from the outset, ensuring that sustainability is a primary consideration in all phases of an asset's life.

The circular economy offers a revolutionary framework for green maintenance, focusing on reuse, recycling and waste reduction at all stages of a product's life cycle. Green maintenance will continue to increasingly adopt circular principles, seeking not only to repair and maintain, but also to reimagine how resources can be conserved and revalued.

These practices could include activities such as rebuilding equipment, using recycled materials in repairs, and designing products with disassembly and recycling in mind, creating a closed loop that minimizes environmental impact.

While the future of green maintenance is certainly bright, it is also full of challenges. Rapidly evolving technologies require significant investments in training and development, as well as continuous adaptation to new regulations and sustainability standards. However, these same technologies offer unprecedented opportunities to innovate and lead in creating a more sustainable future.

The widespread adoption of green maintenance, driven by IoTA, AI and the circular economy, will not only improve operational efficiency and reduce environmental impact, but also strengthen the resilience of organizations in the face of global challenges such as climate change and resource scarcity.

As we move towards this future, it is crucial that organizations, governments and society at large work closely together to leverage these technologies, not only to improve the maintenance of our assets and infrastructure, but also to ensure a legacy of sustainability for future generations.

CHAPTER 2: KEY ASPECTS OF GREEN MAINTENANCE

SUSTAINABILITY IN MAINTENANCE

Sustainability in maintenance is establishing itself as a fundamental principle for modern operations in a variety of sectors, from manufacturing to public infrastructure and building management.

This approach not only seeks operational efficiency and reduced environmental impact, but also aligns with a broader commitment to social responsibility and sustainable development.

By integrating sustainable practices into maintenance, organizations can make a significant contribution to environmental protection while improving their performance and reputation.

One of the cornerstones of sustainability in maintenance is resource conservation. This involves implementing technologies and procedures that optimize the use of water, energy and raw materials, minimizing waste throughout the value chain.

For example, the installation of energy-efficient LED lighting systems and process automation can significantly reduce energy consumption.

Similarly, the use of predictive maintenance techniques can extend the useful life of equipment, ensuring that the resources invested in its manufacture are used to the maximum.

Reducing the emission of waste and pollutants is another critical goal of sustainability in maintenance. This is achieved not only through the adoption of cleaner and more efficient processes, but also through the conscious design of products and systems that are easier to maintain, repair or recycle.

The implementation of a solid waste management program, including segregation, recycling and proper disposal of waste, is a practical example of how maintenance operations can minimize their environmental footprint.

Social equity is an essential component of sustainable maintenance practices. This involves ensuring that maintenance operations are not only environmentally responsible, but also contribute to the economic and social well-being of the community and workers.

For example, the adoption of fair labor practices and the inclusion of the local community in maintenance projects can foster a more equitable and sustainable work environment.

The transition to the use of renewable energies is essential to reduce dependence on fossil fuels and mitigate climate change.

In the context of maintenance, this may involve installing solar panels on buildings, using biofuels in machinery or adopting electric vehicles for maintenance tasks. These actions not only reduce carbon emissions, but can also offer long-term economic savings.

Energy audits are valuable tools for identifying areas for improvement in the energy efficiency of maintenance operations. By systematically assessing energy consumption and material flows, organizations can uncover opportunities to optimize their processes and reduce their environmental impact.

ENERGY EFFICIENCY AND RESOURCE MANAGEMENT

Energy efficiency and resource management are fundamental to the green maintenance strategy of any organization aware of the environmental impact of its operations. These practices not only seek to minimize the consumption of energy and natural resources, but also to optimize maintenance processes to ensure their long-term sustainability.

Through equipment upgrades, preventive maintenance, resource audits and the implementation of sustainable practices, organizations can achieve a more efficient and responsible operation.

Replacing old and obsolete equipment with more energy-efficient models is a crucial step towards improving energy efficiency. Technological advances in equipment manufacturing have led to the availability of machines that use significantly less energy to perform the same tasks or even improve performance.

Investing in this equipment not only reduces energy consumption and operating costs, but can also reduce greenhouse gas emissions associated with energy production.

Regular preventive maintenance is essential to ensure the optimal and efficient operation of equipment. By proactively inspecting and repairing equipment before it fails, organizations can avoid wasted energy caused by inefficiently operating machines.

In addition, preventive maintenance can extend the useful life of equipment, reducing the need for frequent replacements and the environmental impact associated with manufacturing new equipment.

Conducting resource audits is an effective method to evaluate the consumption of water, energy and other critical inputs in maintenance operations. These audits can identify areas where efficiency can be improved, such as leaks in water systems, inefficiencies in thermal insulation or excessive energy use in certain processes.

By addressing these issues, organizations can significantly reduce their resource consumption and reduce their environmental footprint.

The implementation of rainwater harvesting systems and recycling solutions are examples of sustainable practices, which can complement energy efficiency and resource management in maintenance. These systems not only help conserve important resources, but also promote a more sustainable resource use cycle.

For example, collected rainwater can be used for irrigation or cooling processes, reducing the demand for potable water. Similarly, recycling solutions can minimize the amount of waste generated by maintenance operations, fostering a circular economy.

WASTE REDUCTION AND MANAGEMENT

Waste reduction and management have become essential components of a sustainable operation, reflecting a commitment to both environmental preservation and economic efficiency. Effective waste management strategies not only reduce pollution and the use of natural resources, but can also result in significant savings and the creation of new business opportunities.

In this context, process optimization and the implementation of recycling programs represent fundamental steps towards a more sustainable waste management.

Reviewing and modifying operating procedures to minimize waste generation is a proactive approach to waste management. This approach involves evaluating production and maintenance chains to identify where and how waste can be reduced.

For example, digitizing processes can significantly reduce the use of paper, while redesigning packaging can reduce waste material. Optimization can also involve the reuse of certain materials at different stages of the production process, thus minimizing the need for new inputs and waste generation.

Establishing effective separation and recycling systems in the workplace is crucial to successful waste management. These programs not only facilitate the recovery and recycling of valuable materials, but also foster a culture of sustainability among employees.

By implementing clearly labeled recycling garbage cans and providing training on proper recycling practices, organizations can ensure effective waste separation, which facilitates waste treatment and minimizes the volume of waste sent to landfills.

Adopting a circular economy strategy, where resources are kept in use for as long as possible, plays a vital role in reducing the waste footprint.

This involves designing products so that they can be easily repaired, reused or recycled at the end of their useful life. In addition, by investing in technologies that enable the transformation of waste into new products or energy, companies can close the cycle of their resources, thereby reducing the demand for raw materials and the generation of waste.

Beyond the environmental benefits, effective waste management offers significant economic advantages. Reducing waste generation can reduce the costs associated with waste disposal, while recycling programs can generate revenue through the sale of recyclable materials.

In addition, by adopting cleaner and more efficient production practices, companies can improve their competitiveness in the marketplace, meeting the growing demand for sustainable products and services.

USE OF CLEAN AND RENEWABLE TECHNOLOGIES

The transition towards the use of clean technologies and renewable energies represents a crucial evolution in maintenance practices, in line with the global commitment to reduce dependence on fossil fuels and minimize environmental impact. This transition involves not only the adoption of more sustainable energy sources, such as solar and wind, but also the exploration of innovative solutions in biomass and geothermal energy, as well as the implementation of advanced automation systems and the use of environmentally friendly materials.

These approaches offer a promising route to cleaner, more efficient and environmentally responsible operations.

The installation of solar panels and wind turbines enables organizations to generate their own clean energy, significantly reducing their carbon footprint. These increasingly efficient and affordable technologies can provide sustainable electricity for a wide range of maintenance operations, from lighting facilities to running machinery.

In addition, the surplus energy produced can be sold to the grid, generating additional income or offsetting energy consumption costs.

Biomass and geothermal energy present viable alternatives for more sustainable heating and cooling systems. Biomass, which uses organic materials as an energy source, can be a renewable option for heat and power production, while geothermal energy harnesses heat from underground, offering an efficient, low-impact solution for climate control of buildings and facilities.

These technologies not only decrease dependence on fossil fuels, but can also offer lower long-term operating costs.

The integration of automated systems and Internet of Things (IoT) devices into maintenance practices enables more efficient management of energy consumption. These systems can continuously monitor energy usage, automatically adjusting equipment operation to maximize efficiency.

For example, lighting and air conditioning can be controlled according to occupancy or ambient conditions, minimizing energy waste.

The selection of low environmental impact materials for repairs and maintenance is another pillar in the adoption of clean technologies. This includes the use of non-toxic paints and solvents, recycled or sustainable building materials, and energy-efficient components.

The use of these materials not only reduces the direct environmental impact of maintenance operations, but also contributes to the creation of healthier and more sustainable environments.

CHAPTER 3: TOOLS AND TECHNOLOGIES IN GREEN MAINTENANCE

In the current era, characterized by a growing awareness of sustainability and the environmental impact of our activities, green maintenance has established itself as an essential practice for organizations around the world.

This chapter focuses on advanced tools and technologies that facilitate the diagnosis, monitoring and efficient management of resources, contributing significantly to environmental sustainability.

ENVIRONMENTAL DIAGNOSIS AND MONITORING

Environmental diagnostics and monitoring are fundamental pillars of green maintenance, enabling organizations to understand and manage their environmental impact.

Applied Technologies: Geographic Information Systems (GIS): They allow the analysis of spatial environmental data to make informed decisions on resource management and territorial planning.

Drones and Satellites: They provide aerial imagery and data for monitoring large areas, useful in assessing vegetation cover, detecting environmental changes and monitoring critical infrastructure.

Benefits:

Prevention and Mitigation: Early detection of environmental anomalies, helps prevent damage and mitigate negative impacts.

Resource Optimization: Accurate data enables more efficient management of resources, reducing waste.

INTELLIGENT SENSORS AND DEVICES FOR ENERGY SAVING

Smart sensors and devices transform green maintenance through automation and precise control of energy consumption.

Occupancy Sensors: Automatically adjust lighting and HVAC based on human presence, optimizing energy consumption.

Smart Thermostats: Learn from usage patterns and adjust heating and cooling, to maximize efficiency.

Impact

Reduced Energy Consumption: These devices can significantly reduce energy consumption, contributing to environmental sustainability and reduced operating costs.

Improved Comfort and Productivity: Maintaining the optimum environment contributes to occupant well-being and productivity in work and residential spaces.

ENERGY MANAGEMENT SYSTEMS (EMS)

Energy management systems (EMS) are crucial for monitoring, controlling and optimizing energy use in green maintenance operations.

Integration with Renewable Energy: BMS can be integrated with renewable energy systems, such as solar or wind, for efficient energy supply management.

Analysis and Reporting: Provides detailed analysis of energy consumption, identifying areas for improvement and helping to formulate consumption reduction strategies.

Improved Efficiency: EMSs contribute to greater energy efficiency by identifying and eliminating waste.

Regulatory Compliance: Facilitate compliance with energy efficiency and sustainability regulations.

INNOVATIONS IN ECOLOGICAL TOOLS AND EQUIPMENT

Continuous innovation in eco-friendly tools and equipment is revolutionizing green maintenance, offering more sustainable and efficient solutions.

Energy Efficient Tools: Equipment and tools designed to minimize energy consumption without compromising efficiency.

Green Materials: Development of more sustainable materials for the manufacture of tools and equipment, reducing the carbon footprint.

Reduced Environmental Impact: The use of environmentally friendly tools and equipment significantly reduces the environmental impact of maintenance activities.

Economic Sustainability: Although the initial investment may be higher, the long-term savings in energy costs and the reduced need for replacement make these innovations economically viable options.

CHAPTER 4: MONITORING, METRICS AND CONTINUOUS IMPROVEMENT

This chapter focuses on monitoring, metrics and continuous improvement, which are critical to the success of green maintenance. This trilogy not only allows organizations to evaluate the effectiveness of their sustainability strategies, but also to identify areas for improvement and adapt to change with agility.

Delving deeper into these elements reveals how adopting a systematic, data-driven approach can drive operational efficiency and environmental sustainability.

SELECTION OF KEY PERFORMANCE INDICATORS (KPIS)

The selection of Key Performance Indicators (KPIs) plays a critical role in the management and optimization of green maintenance. These KPIs should not only reflect efficiency and savings goals, but also encapsulate the organization's commitment to environmental sustainability.

Choosing the right KPIs is a process that requires a thorough understanding of the organization's operations as well as its environmental and social impacts.

KPIs in the context of green maintenance should be designed to encourage continuous reflection on how maintenance practices can be improved to be more sustainable.

This involves considering not only immediate results, such as reduced energy consumption, but also long-term impacts, such as conservation of natural resources and reduction of the organization's overall ecological footprint.

For example, a KPI that measures water use efficiency can not only lead to reduced water consumption, but also inspire the adoption of water recycling systems in operations.

For KPIs to be effective, they must be both measurable and

relevant. This means that each KPI must have clear metrics that can be quantified and compared over time.

In addition, KPIs should be relevant to the organization's specific sustainability objectives. Relevance ensures that resources and efforts are focused on areas that will truly impact the company's environmental performance.

KPIs should be designed not only to measure performance, but also to drive concrete actions. This means that the results of KPIs must be able to inform decisions and improvement strategies.

For example, a KPI that measures the percentage of waste recycled can inspire the implementation of more effective waste segregation programs or the search for more efficient recycling partners.

Energy Consumption Reduction: Measure the reduction in energy use across all operations, encouraging the implementation of more efficient technologies and energy conservation practices.

Percentage of Waste Recycled: This KPI can encourage the adoption of recycling practices and the search for sustainable alternatives for waste management.

Carbon footprint reduction: Measure the reduction in CO_2 emissions associated with the organization's operations, encouraging the adoption of renewable energy and cleaner operating practices.

Water Use Efficiency: This KPI emphasizes the importance of conserving water, an increasingly scarce resource, by measuring the amount of water used per unit of production or service.

Employee Satisfaction and Well-Being: Although not directly related to environmental impact, this KPI reflects the importance of sustainable maintenance practices in creating a healthy and safe work environment, which is critical to long-term sustainability.

DATA MONITORING AND ANALYSIS TOOLS

In the field of green maintenance, the ability to efficiently monitor resource use and analyze operational data is essential to optimize performance and minimize environmental impact.

With the advancement of technology, monitoring and data analysis tools have become increasingly sophisticated, offering unprecedented opportunities to improve operational sustainability.

Intelligent Building Management Systems (BMS) are centralized platforms that control and monitor a building's infrastructure systems, such as lighting, HVAC, and energy systems.

These systems not only enable more efficient management of energy consumption, but also facilitate preventive maintenance by alerting to potential system failures or inefficiencies. By providing detailed data on energy usage and operating conditions, BMSs enable managers to optimize operations and significantly reduce resource consumption.

Internet of Things (IoT) devices have revolutionized the way maintenance data is collected and analyzed. These devices, which can be sensors, smart meters or automated controls, collect real-time data on equipment performance and resource usage.

This information enables immediate operational adjustments and informed decisions on maintenance and resource management, which can lead to significant reductions in energy and water consumption, as well as waste generation.

Data analytics platforms and business intelligence software transform the large volumes of data collected by BMS systems and IoT devices into actionable information for decision making. Using advanced algorithms and machine learning techniques, these tools can identify patterns, predict trends and provide recommendations to improve efficiency and sustainability.

The ability to analyze data, from multiple sources in aggregate, provides a holistic view of operations, highlighting areas of inefficiency and opportunities for improvement that might be overlooked without data analysis.

The integration of these monitoring and analysis technologies offers multiple benefits for green maintenance, including:

Resource Use Optimization: The ability to monitor and adjust in real time the consumption of resources such as energy and water can lead to significant savings and a smaller environmental footprint.

Predictive Maintenance: Early identification of potential problems in equipment and systems can prevent costly failures and reduce the need for corrective maintenance.

Data-Driven Decisions: Detailed analysis of operational data, enables informed decisions, which can improve operational efficiency and environmental sustainability.

Transparency and Accountability: Data collection and analysis, provides a solid basis for reporting to stakeholders, on environmental performance and operational efficiency.

FOSTERING A CULTURE OF CONTINUOUS IMPROVEMENT

Fostering a culture of continuous improvement is a fundamental pillar for any organization that aspires to integrate sustainability into the core of its operations. This holistic approach not only improves operational and environmental performance, but also drives innovation and organizational resilience.

By cultivating this culture, organizations can adapt more effectively to market changes, evolving environmental regulations and societal expectations, ensuring their long-term viability.

The success of continuous improvement in sustainability depends on the involvement of all levels of the organization. Top management must lead by example, setting clear sustainability goals and making a personal commitment to them.

This includes integrating sustainable practices into the company's mission and vision, as well as into its strategic decision-making processes. For operational staff, it is crucial to understand how their roles and responsibilities contribute to these objectives, fostering their commitment and motivation to implement sustainable practices in their daily activities.

Sustainability training programs are essential to equip employees with the necessary knowledge and skills to effectively contribute to the organization's sustainability objectives.

These programs should be inclusive, ranging from a basic understanding of sustainability principles to specific improvement techniques in areas such as energy efficiency, waste management and resource use.

Continuous training helps keep staff up-to-date on best practices and emerging technologies, fostering a mindset of constant learning and adaptation.

Implementing incentive systems can be an effective strategy to motivate the adoption of sustainable practices. These can range from recognition and awards to bonuses and promotions based on performance in sustainability initiatives.

Incentives not only reward individual and team efforts, but also highlight the importance the organization places on sustainability, reinforcing its value as a shared goal.

Internal and external collaboration platforms are crucial for sharing knowledge, experiences and best practices in sustainability. Internally, these platforms can facilitate communication between different departments and organizational levels, promoting a unified approach to sustainability objectives.

Externally, collaboration with other organizations, educational institutions and stakeholders can provide new perspectives and innovative solutions to sustainability challenges.

To sustain a culture of continuous improvement, it is vital to establish regular evaluation and feedback processes. This includes regularly reviewing sustainability KPIs, conducting internal audits and gathering feedback from employees and other stakeholders.

These processes not only allow us to measure progress towards sustainability objectives, but also identify areas for improvement and opportunities for innovation.

IMPLEMENTATION AND EVALUATION

Implementation and evaluation, within the framework of continuous improvement and sustainability, is a dynamic process that requires constant attention and deep organizational commitment. This iterative cycle not only enables organizations to be more resilient and adaptive to emerging challenges, but also positions them to lead in innovation and sustainability.

By breaking down this process, several critical phases can be identified that facilitate the effective integration of sustainable practices into the core of maintenance operations.

Assessment is the starting point of this cycle, where an in-depth analysis of the current state of the organization's maintenance and sustainability practices is performed. This phase involves reviewing existing KPIs, measuring performance against these indicators and conducting energy and resource audits to identify areas of inefficiency. The assessment should be comprehensive, covering not only technical and operational aspects, but also evaluating the environmental, economic and social impact of current practices.

Based on the results of the assessment, the planning phase involves the development of strategies and action plans aimed at addressing the identified areas for improvement.

This includes defining new KPIs or reviewing existing ones

to better align them with sustainability objectives, identifying innovative technologies and practices that can be implemented, and developing a training plan to ensure that all members of the organization are equipped to contribute to sustainability objectives.

Implementation of the strategies and action plans developed in the planning phase is carried out in the action phase. This may involve introducing new technologies or processes, making modifications to facilities or equipment to improve energy efficiency, or implementing recycling and waste management programs.

During this phase, it is vital to maintain clear and open communication with all stakeholders to ensure understanding and commitment to the new initiatives.

The review phase closes the cycle, providing an opportunity to reflect on the success of the strategies implemented and gather feedback from all stakeholders. This involves re-measuring performance against KPIs, assessing the environmental, economic and social impact of actions taken, and gathering feedback on processes and results.

The information gathered during this phase is crucial to inform the next round of evaluation, ensuring that the continuous improvement process is truly iterative.

Effective implementation and evaluation in the context of continuous improvement and sustainability requires a holistic view and a collaborative approach.

By adopting this iterative cycle, organizations can ensure that their maintenance strategies are not only environmentally sustainable, but also economically viable and benefit society as a whole.

This approach not only enhances organizational resilience and adaptive capacity, but also fosters innovation, enabling organizations to lead in a business environment that is increasingly focused on sustainability.

CHAPTER 5: GREEN MAINTENANCE AND ASSET MANAGEMENT

At the heart of any corporate sustainability strategy lies the efficient management of physical assets through green maintenance. This approach not only extends the useful life of equipment and reduces waste, but also ensures that operations are conducted in an environmentally responsible manner.

This chapter explores how the integration of green maintenance into asset management can transform traditional operations into sustainable practices, fostering a corporate culture that prioritizes environmental performance along with operational efficiency.

INTEGRATING GREEN MAINTENANCE INTO PHYSICAL ASSET MANAGEMENT

The integration of green maintenance into physical asset management is an increasingly crucial strategy for organizations seeking not only to maximize efficiency and reduce costs, but also to meet their environmental and social responsibilities.

This holistic approach to sustainability in asset management involves reconsidering every aspect of the asset life cycle, from acquisition and use to maintenance and eventual decommissioning or recycling, incorporating sustainable practices at every step of the process.

Integrating sustainability begins with asset procurement. Adopting sustainable procurement policies means selecting equipment and materials that not only meet operational requirements, but are also energy efficient, durable and, as far as possible, sustainably manufactured.

This involves assessing the environmental impact of assets throughout their life cycle, including the carbon emissions generated during their production, operation and final disposal.

Preventive maintenance plays a key role in extending the useful life of assets and minimizing their environmental impact. Well planned and executed maintenance programs can prevent unexpected failures, reduce energy consumption and reduce the need for frequent replacement of parts and equipment.

This not only contributes to environmental sustainability, but also optimizes financial resources by reducing long-term operating and maintenance costs.

Improved efficiency, through the implementation of green maintenance practices, has a direct impact on cost reduction.

By optimizing energy use, minimizing waste and improving resource efficiency, organizations can experience a significant decrease in operating expenses. In addition, the use of sustainable technologies and materials can qualify organizations for tax incentives and government grants, providing additional financial benefits.

In a world where environmental regulations are becoming increasingly stringent, adopting green maintenance practices ensures that organizations not only comply with these regulations, but often exceed them. This can avoid costly fines and penalties, while enhancing corporate reputation.

A strong reputation for sustainability can be a key differentiator in the marketplace, attracting customers, investors and talent who value environmental responsibility.

Effective integration of green maintenance into physical asset management requires a continuous approach to implementation and evaluation. This involves establishing processes to regularly review the environmental performance of assets, adjusting maintenance policies as necessary, and constantly exploring new technologies and practices that can further improve sustainability.

Continuous evaluation ensures that maintenance practices not only respond to current needs, but also adapt to future challenges and opportunities.

EQUIPMENT LIFETIME OPTIMIZATION WITH SUSTAINABLE APPROACHES

Adopting sustainable approaches to equipment maintenance and management is critical for organizations seeking not only to maximize operational and financial efficiency, but also to minimize their environmental impact.

Optimizing the useful life of equipment through strategies such as predictive maintenance, condition-based maintenance and refurbishment represents a significant opportunity to move towards more sustainable operations.

These practices not only extend the effective use of assets, but also contribute to a more responsible management of natural resources and waste reduction.

Predictive maintenance, powered by advanced technologies such as the Internet of Things (IoT) and data analytics, is a key pillar in optimizing equipment lifetime.

Through real-time monitoring and predictive analytics, it is possible to identify early signs of wear or potential equipment failures before they become major problems.

This anticipation allows precise and timely interventions, avoiding unplanned shutdowns and extending the useful life of the equipment.

In addition, predictive maintenance optimizes the use of resources by ensuring that maintenance is only performed when it is really necessary, rather than following a fixed schedule over time, which could result in unnecessary or late interventions.

E he refurbishment of equipment and components are valuable strategies to extend their useful life and maximize the investment in assets.

These processes involve restoring used or damaged equipment to "as new" condition, often at a significantly lower cost than purchasing new. In addition to the economic advantage, refurbishment reduces the demand for new materials and the energy required to produce new equipment, contributing to resource efficiency and reducing the carbon footprint associated with manufacturing new assets.

One of the most significant contributions of sustainable approaches to equipment maintenance is the reduction of waste. By extending the useful life of equipment, the frequency of disposal and replacement is reduced, which in turn reduces the amount of waste generated.

This not only has a positive impact on the environment, but also helps organizations comply with stricter environmental regulations and improve their corporate image with consumers and stakeholders who value sustainability.

Optimizing the useful life of equipment through sustainable practices also improves efficiency in the use of materials and energy. By maximizing the performance of existing assets, organizations can reduce their dependence on new resources, minimizing their environmental impact and ensuring a more responsible use of natural resources.

This aligns with circular economy principles, where the goal is to keep products and materials in use for as long as possible and to regenerate natural systems.

ENVIRONMENTAL PERFORMANCE MEASUREMENT AND TRACKING

Measuring and monitoring environmental performance is central to the strategy of any organization committed to sustainability. By establishing environmental Key Performance Indicators (KPIs) and adopting Environmental Management Systems (EMS), companies can not only evaluate the effectiveness of their green housekeeping initiatives, but also identify opportunities to improve their environmental performance over time.

These efforts contribute significantly to optimizing processes, reducing costs and strengthening corporate reputation.

The definition of environmental KPIs allows organizations to concretely measure the impact of their operations on the environment. These indicators must be specific, measurable, achievable, relevant and time-bound (SMART) to be effective. Examples of environmental KPIs may include:

Energy Consumption Reduction: Measures the efficiency of energy use in operations and can help identify opportunities to implement more efficient solutions.

Waste Recycling Rate: This indicator measures the percentage of waste recycled with respect to total waste generated, highlighting the effectiveness of waste management policies.

Water Consumption per Production Unit: Allows to evaluate the efficient use of water and promote practices that minimize the waste of this vital resource.

Carbon footprint: Calculates the total CO_2 equivalent emissions generated by the organization's operations, being crucial for emission reduction strategies.

These KPIs provide a solid basis for informed decision making and the implementation of maintenance practices that are not only sustainable, but also optimize the use of resources.

EMSs are structured frameworks that enable organizations to monitor, control and continuously improve their environmental impact. Implementing an EMS, such as ISO 14001, helps companies to:

Standardize Processes: Ensuring that all operations are performed in a manner that minimizes environmental impact.

Regulatory Compliance: Keeping up to date with environmental laws and regulations, avoiding penalties and fines.

Continuous Improvement: Through regular review and updating of policies and procedures to improve environmental performance.

The adoption of an EMS fosters an organizational culture that prioritizes sustainability, involving employees at all levels and encouraging their participation in the identification and implementation of sustainable practices.

Ongoing measurement of environmental performance brings numerous benefits to organizations, including:

Continuous Improvement: Identifying areas for improvement allows us to adjust strategies and operations to more effectively achieve sustainability objectives.

Data-Driven Decision Making: Data obtained through measurement and monitoring enables detailed analysis and informed decisions that support sustainability objectives.

Transparency and Credibility: Publishing and sharing sustainability achievements improves the company's public image and strengthens trust among customers, investors and other stakeholders.

Innovation: Constant review of environmental performance, can reveal opportunities to innovate in products, services, and processes, keeping the organization at the forefront of sustainability

CHAPTER 6: STANDARDS, CERTIFICATIONS AND POLICIES, IN GREEN MAINTENANCE

Green maintenance, essential for progress towards corporate and environmental sustainability, is strongly influenced by a framework of legislation, certifications and corporate policies.

This chapter delves into how these regulations drive sustainable maintenance practices, certifications that validate green efforts, and internal policies that companies can adopt to commit to sustainability.

EVOLUTION OF ENVIRONMENTAL REGULATIONS: GLOBAL AND REGIONAL IMPACT

Environmental regulations have undergone a significant evolution over the last decades, reflecting a growing recognition of the importance of protecting the environment and promoting sustainable practices in all sectors of the economy.

At the global level, agreements such as the Kyoto Protocol and the Paris Agreement have established frameworks for reducing greenhouse gas emissions, setting a precedent for collective action against climate change.

Regionally, the European Union has been noted for its extensive body of environmental legislation, including the REACH Regulation, which controls chemicals produced or imported into the EU, and the Energy Efficiency Directive, which sets targets for improving energy efficiency in member states.

These regulations not only seek to protect the environment, but also to encourage a transition to greener and more sustainable economies.

Maintenance practices in all types of industries and companies have been directly influenced by these evolutions in regulations. For example, equipment and systems maintenance is now performed with a greater focus on energy efficiency and pollution reduction, adopting clean technologies and processes that minimize environmental impact.

DIRECT IMPACT OF LEGISLATION ON GREEN MAINTENANCE

Environmental legislation has had a direct impact on the adoption of green maintenance practices in several sectors.

A notable example is the construction sector, where LEED (Leadership in Energy and Environmental Design) certification has transformed construction and maintenance practices, encouraging the use of sustainable materials and energy efficiency in buildings.

In industry, legislation such as the EU's Industrial Emissions Directive has prompted companies to adopt cleaner technologies and maintenance processes that reduce air, water and soil pollution.

This not only helps companies to comply with legal requirements, but also to improve their public image and reduce long-term costs through improved efficiency.

CHALLENGES AND OPPORTUNITIES

While environmental regulations present challenges for companies, especially in terms of upfront costs and adapting to new standards, they also offer numerous opportunities for innovation and leadership in sustainability.

Compliance with these regulations can drive companies to explore new technologies and green maintenance practices, opening avenues to market differentiation and competitive advantage.

In addition, exceeding the minimum requirements of environmental legislation can enable companies to position themselves as leaders in sustainability, attracting customers and business partners who value responsible business practices.

This can translate into tangible economic benefits, such as increased market share and greater customer loyalty, the latter of which is increasingly important for public or private companies.

GREEN CERTIFICATIONS AND ECO LABELS

In the field of green maintenance and corporate sustainability, green certifications and eco-labels play a crucial role. These distinctions are internationally recognized and serve as a barometer to measure an organization's commitment to sustainable practices and respect for the environment.

Among the most influential certifications are LEED (Leadership in Energy and Environmental Design), ISO 14001 (Environmental Management Systems), and ENERGY STAR, each addressing different aspects of environmental performance and sustainability.

Introduction to Main Certifications

-LEED is a globally recognized sustainable building certification system that assesses elements such as energy efficiency, water use, indoor air quality, and innovative design.

-ISO 14001 is an international standard that specifies the requirements for an effective environmental management system (EMS), enabling organizations to improve their environmental performance through a process of planning, implementation, review and continual improvement.

-ENERGY STAR is a program that identifies and certifies products, buildings and companies that meet high energy efficiency standards, helping to save costs and protect the environment.

PROCESS TO OBTAIN CERTIFICATIONS

The path to green certification involves several steps, from the initial assessment to the final audit:

Initial Assessment: Identification of areas for improvement and establishment of sustainability goals, in accordance with the desired certification criteria.

Planning and Implementation: Development of a plan to bring operations, maintenance practices and policies in line with required standards. This may include investments in more efficient technology, improvements in waste management, or employee training on sustainable practices.

Documentation and Follow-up: Compilation of evidence and documentation of compliance with certification criteria, as well as continuous monitoring of environmental performance.

Final Audit: Once the measures have been implemented, a certifying entity performs an exhaustive evaluation to verify compliance. If the criteria are met, certification is granted.

IMPACT OF CERTIFICATIONS

Green certifications not only validate an organization's sustainability efforts, but also offer tangible and intangible benefits, including:

Improved Corporate Reputation: Certifications act as a seal of approval that enhances the company's public image, strengthening its brand and attractiveness in the marketplace.

Increased Operational Efficiency: The adoption of sustainable maintenance practices leads to greater efficiency in the use of resources, which can result in significant savings in operating and energy costs.

Tax or Regulatory Incentives: In many jurisdictions, certified companies may benefit from tax incentives, subsidies, or favorable regulatory conditions.

Competitive Advantage: Certification can differentiate a company in the marketplace, attracting customers and business partners who value sustainability.

CORPORATE POLICIES FOR THE PROMOTION OF GREEN MAINTENANCE

The adoption of corporate policies focused on green maintenance is essential for companies committed to sustainability and environmental responsibility.

These policies not only reflect an organization's commitment to environmental stewardship, but can also improve operational efficiency, reduce costs and strengthen brand image. The following are guidelines and examples of how companies can promote green housekeeping through effective internal policies.

Development of Internal Policies for Green Maintenance

Companies can initiate the development of green maintenance policies by integrating sustainable objectives into their corporate mission and vision. This process begins with the commitment of top management and the inclusion of sustainability as a central pillar of business strategy.

The following are key steps in developing these policies:

Current Situation Analysis: Conduct an environmental diagnosis to understand current operations and their impact on the environment. This analysis can help identify areas for improvement and establish a starting point for policy development.

Setting Goals and Objectives: Define clear and achievable goals related to sustainability and green maintenance. These goals can range from reducing energy and water consumption to implementing recycling and waste management practices.

Policy Development: Draft policies that reflect the company's sustainable objectives, including specific procedures for green housekeeping. It is essential that these policies are clear, detailed and stipulate specific responsibilities within the organization.

Training and Awareness: Implement training programs to ensure that all employees understand green maintenance policies and their role in achieving sustainable objectives.

Monitoring and Evaluation: Establish monitoring and evaluation systems, to measure progress toward sustainability objectives, allowing for policy adjustments as needed.

Case Studies of Successful Green Maintenance Policies

IKEA: IKEA is known worldwide not only for its affordable, intelligently designed furniture and home products, but also for its commitment to sustainability. The company has implemented significant policies and practices to minimize its environmental impact and encourage more sustainable behavior among its consumers and in its supply chain.

Key aspects of IKEA's sustainability policy:

Use of Sustainable Materials:

IKEA strives to use renewable or recycled resources in its products. A prime example is its commitment to use only wood from more sustainable sources, such as certified or recycled forests.

They are also increasing the use of recycled materials and alternative raw materials, such as recycled plastics and biomaterials.

Circular Design and Waste Reduction:

The company adopts circular design principles, ensuring that products are durable, can be reused, remanufactured, and ultimately recycled.

IKEA also works to reduce waste in its operations and has implemented a zero waste initiative in its stores and restaurants, including efforts to minimize food waste.

Renewable Energy and Energy Efficiency:

IKEA is committed to using 100% renewable energy in its global operations, investing in solar and wind energy solutions at its properties.

The company also strives to improve energy efficiency in all its stores, warehouses and production centers.

Corporate Social Responsibility:

IKEA promotes fair and safe working conditions throughout its supply chain and strives to be a good neighbor in the communities where it operates.

The company also participates in various global initiatives to support human rights and vulnerable communities, including refugee support programs and women's empowerment projects.

Transportation and Logistics Initiatives:

IKEA seeks to reduce the environmental impact of its logistics operations by optimizing transportation routes and increasing the use of low-emission or electric vehicles.

Consumer Participation:

IKEA encourages consumers to adopt more sustainable practices at home through products that promote energy savings, water efficiency and waste reduction.

The company offers solutions for customers to recycle or repair products, and sells products that facilitate a more sustainable lifestyle, such as food storage solutions that reduce waste.

Patagonia: A U.S.-based company that sells outdoor clothing and equipment, Patagonia is widely recognized for its deep commitment to sustainability and environmental responsibility. Its business philosophy focuses on minimizing its environmental impact and using its platform to promote environmental conservation and sustainable solutions.

Sustainable Materials:

Patagonia uses organic, recycled and low environmental impact materials. For example, its cotton clothing line has been 100% organic since 1996.

In addition, they have increased the use of recycled materials in their products, including recycled polyester and recycled wool.

Environmental Impact Reduction:

The company has implemented practices to reduce water, energy and chemical use in its production chain.

It strives to improve energy efficiency and has invested in renewable energy sources for its operations.

Repair and Reuse Initiatives:

Patagonia encourages product repair through its Worn Wear program, where it sells used and repaired clothing to extend the useful life of its products and reduce the need for new resources.

They offer guides and resources for consumers to repair their own clothing, promoting a circular economy.

Activism and Donations:

The company is known for its activism on environmental and social issues. It has participated in numerous campaigns to protect threatened lands and ecosystems and to promote sustainable environmental policies.

Patagonia donates 1% of its total sales to environmental organizations through its "1% for the Planet" initiative, contributing millions of dollars to conservation causes.

Transparency and Ethics:

Patagonia is committed to complete transparency in its sourcing and production practices. They regularly publish detailed reports on their environmental impacts and progress.

The company ensures that everyone in its supply chain is treated ethically and fairly.

Influence in the industry:

Patagonia seeks to influence other companies to adopt more sustainable practices. They have helped establish and support several industry groups and coalitions focused on sustainability.

These cases show how green maintenance policies can be integrated into business operations to reduce environmental impact and, at the same time, contribute positively to brand image and profitability.

TOOLS AND RESOURCES FOR GREEN MAINTENANCE POLICY DEVELOPMENT

Sustainability and Carbon Footprint Assessments

Before implementing any policy, it is crucial to understand the company's starting point in terms of sustainability. Tools such as sustainability assessment and carbon footprint calculations allow companies to measure their current environmental impacts.

Platforms such as Carbon Footprint and The Global Reporting Initiative offer frameworks and tools for conducting these assessments, helping companies to identify priority areas for action.

Environmental Management Systems (EMS)

EMSs, such as ISO 14001, provide a framework for companies to plan, implement, monitor and continually improve their green housekeeping policies. Implementing an EMS can help a company manage its environmental impacts in a systematic way, ensuring that green maintenance policies are integrated at all levels of the organization.

Resource Management Tools

To effectively manage the consumption of resources, such as water and energy, there are specific monitoring and management tools, such as Energy Star Portfolio Manager, that allow companies to track and analyze their consumption. These tools can identify areas of inefficiency and help set clear targets for reducing consumption.

IMPLEMENTATION AND MONITORING OF GREEN MAINTENANCE POLICIES

Staff Training and Commitment

Successful implementation of green maintenance policies requires the commitment of all personnel. Training and awareness programs can help ensure that employees understand their role in implementing these policies and are motivated to contribute to the company's sustainability goals.

Green Technology

The adoption of green technologies, such as efficient LED lighting or intelligent building management systems, can be critical to the implementation of green maintenance policies. These technologies can significantly reduce energy consumption and operating costs while improving a company's environmental performance.

Environmental Key Performance Indicators (KPIs)

Once again, we stress the importance of establishing environmental KPIs, which are crucial for monitoring the effectiveness of green maintenance policies.

These indicators can include measures such as reduction in energy and water consumption, amount of waste recycled or reduction in CO_2 emissions. Sustainability software tools, can help track these KPIs and provide detailed progress reports.

CHAPTER 7: CASE STUDIES AND SUCCESSES

In this chapter, we will explore a series of brief and varied case studies that illustrate the successful implementation of green maintenance practices in a variety of organizations.

These cases will highlight both the benefits gained and the challenges overcome during the process of adopting sustainable practices.

CASE STUDY 1: MANUFACTURING COMPANY

Sustainability has become an imperative for companies in all sectors, including manufacturing.

In this case study, we explore how a fictitious company, EcoManufactura Inc. a leader in the manufacturing industry, embarked on a journey towards sustainability. Through the implementation of innovative energy efficiency and waste management measures, the company not only managed to reduce its operating costs significantly, but also improved its corporate reputation and strengthened its relationships with customers and stakeholders.

BACKGROUND OF ECOMANUFACTURING INC.

EcoManufactura Inc. is a company with more than 20 years in the manufacturing sector, specializing in the production of electronic components. Despite its success, senior management and administration realized the growing importance of adopting sustainable practices to ensure its competitiveness and align with the expectations of customers and regulators.

EVALUATION OF CURRENT PRACTICES

The company began its sustainability journey with a comprehensive assessment of its operations. This included an energy audit, which revealed areas of significant inefficiency, as well as an analysis of waste management, which identified opportunities to improve recycling and reuse of materials.

Implementation of Energy Efficiency Measures

Energy Use Optimization: EcoManufactura Inc. invested in automation technology to optimize energy use in its production processes, resulting in a 25% reduction in energy consumption.

Renewable Energy Sources: The company installed solar panels on the roof of its production plant, covering 40% of its energy needs with solar energy.

Employee Training: Training programs were implemented to raise employee awareness of the importance of energy efficiency and train them in sustainable work practices.

INNOVATION IN WASTE MANAGEMENT

Waste Reduction at Source: EcoManufactura reviewed its production processes, to identify opportunities to reduce waste generation, which included optimizing material utilization and reducing packaging.

Recycling Programs: Recycling programs were established for all recoverable waste, including metals, plastics and paper, achieving a recycling rate of 85%.

Partnerships for Reuse: The company formed partnerships with suppliers and customers to develop programs for the return and reuse of components and materials, extending the useful life of products and reducing the need for raw materials.

RESULTS AND BENEFITS

The adoption of these sustainability initiatives not only resulted in a significant reduction in operating costs for EcoManufactura Inc. but also had a positive impact on its corporate reputation. The company experienced an increase in customer satisfaction and strengthened its relationships with stakeholders, who positively valued its commitment to sustainable practices.

FINANCIAL ANALYSIS

The financial analysis showed that, although the initial investments in energy efficiency technologies and waste management programs were considerable, the savings generated by the reduction in energy consumption and the decrease in waste disposal costs resulted in a return on investment in less than four years.

IMPROVING CORPORATE IMAGE

EcoManufactura Inc. received several sustainability awards, which enhanced its image with customers, investors and the community. In addition, transparency in communicating its sustainability efforts and achievements strengthened customer loyalty and enhanced its attractiveness to talent seeking responsible employers.

CHALLENGES AND LESSONS LEARNED

The road to sustainability was fraught with challenges, from resistance to change within the organization to the need to balance initial investments with long-term benefits.

However, EcoManufactura Inc. learned the importance of fully committing to its sustainability goals and the need to integrate all stakeholders in this process.

CASE STUDY 2: UTILITIES INSTALLATION

Commitment to sustainability and environmental conservation is fundamental for utility facilities, given their direct influence on the community and the environment.

This case study examines AquaServ S.A., a fictitious utility facility that provides water and wastewater treatment to a local community, and how it implemented a green maintenance program to improve the efficiency of its operations and reduce its environmental impact.

BACKGROUND OF AQUASERV S.A.

AquaServ has been operating for more than 30 years, providing essential services, while facing increasing challenges due to aging infrastructure, increased demand for services and pressure to meet stricter environmental regulatory standards.

EVALUATION OF CURRENT PRACTICES

AquaServ began with a comprehensive assessment of its maintenance and operations practices to identify areas for improvement. The assessment revealed several key areas where sustainable practices could be implemented to improve efficiency and reduce environmental impact.

IMPLEMENTATION OF A GREEN MAINTENANCE PROGRAM

AquaServ developed a green maintenance program, focusing on three key areas: energy efficiency, waste management and water conservation.

Energy Efficiency: AquaServ invested in upgrading its infrastructure with more efficient technologies, such as high-efficiency pumps and automated control systems that adjust operations in real time to optimize energy use.

Waste Management: Implemented a comprehensive recycling program to manage waste generated during maintenance and operations, including recycling of materials and proper disposal of hazardous substances.

Water Conservation: Introduced water reuse technologies and system improvements to reduce water loss during treatment and especially in the distribution systems.

RESULTS AND BENEFITS

The implementation of the green maintenance program resulted in a number of tangible benefits to AquaServ and the community it serves:

Regulatory Compliance: AquaServ met and exceeded environmental regulatory standards, avoiding fines and improving its relationship with regulatory authorities.

Cost Savings: Improvements in energy efficiency and reduced water use resulted in significant operational savings, amortizing the initial investment in the green maintenance program.

Community Impact: Water quality improved, and the reduction in energy consumption contributed to a lower community carbon footprint, improving local quality of life.

CHALLENGES AND LESSONS LEARNED

Despite the successes, AquaServ faced challenges in implementing its green maintenance program, including resistance to change within the organization and the need to train employees in new technologies and practices. Lessons learned include the importance of effective communication, ongoing training and commitment to continuous improvement.

CASE STUDY 3: TECHNOLOGY COMPANY

In a world where efficiency and sustainability are becoming essential pillars for business success, innovative technologies offer revolutionary solutions.

This case study explores how TechInnovate, a fictitious company in the technology sector, implemented the Internet of Things (IoT) and Artificial Intelligence (AI) to transform its maintenance operations. We will examine the positive impacts of these technologies on equipment reliability, operational efficiency, energy consumption and maintenance costs.

TECHINNOVATE BACKGROUND

TechInnovate has established itself as a leader in the development of advanced technological solutions. However, it faced significant challenges related to inefficient equipment maintenance and high energy consumption, resulting in high operating costs and considerable environmental impact.

Implementation of IoT and AI Technologies

EVALUATION OF CURRENT PRACTICES

TechInnovate began with a comprehensive assessment of its maintenance operations. This assessment revealed the need to improve real-time data collection and analysis capabilities to predict failures and optimize equipment performance.

IOT INTEGRATION

Real-Time Monitoring: Implementation of IoT sensors in critical equipment to continuously monitor its status and performance.

Energy Efficiency Optimization: Using IoT data, to automatically adjust energy systems and reduce consumption during periods of low demand.

AI APPLICATION

Predictive Analytics: Development of AI models that use collected data to predict failures before they occur, enabling preventive maintenance and reducing downtime.

Operations Optimization: AI algorithms that analyze usage patterns and adjust equipment operation to maximize efficiency and extend equipment life.

RESULTS AND BENEFITS

The integration of IoT and AI transformed TechInnovate's maintenance operations, leading to significant improvements in several key areas:

Reduced Energy Consumption: Intelligent energy management resulted in a 30% reduction in energy consumption.

Decreased Maintenance Costs: Predictive maintenance reduced maintenance costs by 25% by preventing costly failures and optimizing maintenance cycles.

Improved Equipment Reliability: Early detection of potential problems increased equipment reliability by 40%, significantly reducing downtime.

CHALLENGES AND LESSONS LEARNED

Implementing these technologies was not without its challenges. TechInnovate faced obstacles related to integrating existing systems, staff training, and managing large volumes of data. Lessons learned include the importance of a phased approach to technology integration, the need for ongoing training, and the value of a centralized data platform for effective analysis.

CASE STUDY 4: COMMERCIAL BUILDING

At the forefront of sustainable architecture and building maintenance, GreenTower stands out as a business example of how green practices can be integrated into commercial space for the benefit of the environment, tenants and the community at large.

This case study examines the strategies implemented by GreenTower to improve energy efficiency, effectively manage water and select sustainable materials, resulting in reduced operating costs and the creation of a healthy indoor environment.

GREENTOWER BACKGROUND

GreenTower is a state-of-the-art commercial building located in the heart of a dynamic metropolis. Aware of their environmental responsibility and committed to creating a sustainable workspace, GreenTower's managers sought to implement innovative sustainability practices from its conception.

IMPLEMENTATION OF ENERGY EFFICIENCY MEASURES

Energy Efficiency Technologies

LED lighting: GreenTower replaced all traditional lighting systems with LED technology, significantly reducing energy consumption.

Efficient HVAC systems: The installation of highly efficient and energy-efficient heating, ventilation and air conditioning (HVAC) systems contributed to optimized thermal management.

Building Automation: The integration of an intelligent building management system enabled precise control of lighting, temperature and energy consumption, adapting in real time, to the needs of the building.

SUSTAINABLE WATER MANAGEMENT

Rainwater Collection and Use: A rainwater collection system was installed to use the water to irrigate green areas and flush toilets.

Low Flow Devices: To reduce water consumption, low flow devices were installed on faucets, showers and toilets throughout the building.

Gray Water Treatment Systems: GreenTower implemented gray water treatment systems to recycle and reuse water for various applications within the building.

SUSTAINABLE MATERIALS SELECTION

Low Environmental Impact Materials: During renovation and maintenance, GreenTower prioritized the use of environmentally certified materials, including low VOC paints, flooring made from recycled materials and sustainable furnishings.

Efficiency in the Use of Materials: Construction and maintenance practices were adopted to minimize the waste of materials, promoting reuse and recycling whenever possible.

RESULTS AND BENEFITS

The implementation of these sustainability strategies has had a significant impact on GreenTower, resulting in:

Reduced Operating Costs: Energy efficiency and water management measures, resulted in substantial savings in utility costs.

Improved Indoor Environment: The selection of sustainable materials and improvements in air quality and lighting contributed to a healthier and more comfortable work environment for the occupants.

Recognition and Certifications: GreenTower has received several sustainability certifications, reinforcing its reputation as a leader in green building and maintenance practices.

Challenges and Lessons Learned

Implementing these measures was not without its challenges. Managing upfront costs, integrating advanced systems and adapting to tenant needs required a meticulous and strategic approach.

Lessons learned emphasize the importance of careful planning, participation of all stakeholders and adaptability.

Each of these case studies will provide unique insights into how organizations can successfully implement green maintenance practices and overcome the associated challenges.

By studying these inspiring examples, readers will gain valuable insights and lessons, which they can apply in their own organizations, thus moving towards a more sustainable and resilient future.

GENERAL CONCLUSION OF GREEN MAINTENANCE

As we close the pages of this comprehensive journey through green maintenance, we find ourselves at a critical time for both our planet and society. The urgency to adopt sustainable practices in all areas of our lives and work has never been more palpable.

This book has been an in-depth exploration of how maintenance, a function often underestimated in its environmental impact, is transformed into a powerful tool for the well-being of the planet, the economy and our collectivity.

The importance of green maintenance cannot be underestimated. Throughout the chapters, we have unraveled the multiple benefits that these practices bring, not only in terms of environmental preservation, but also in operational efficiency, cost reduction and improved corporate reputation.

We have seen how the implementation of innovative technologies, commitment to continuous improvement and alignment with global sustainability standards can elevate maintenance practices from being just routine tasks to becoming pillars of organizational sustainability.

For readers looking to make a tangible, positive difference, this book offers not only a vision, but also a plan of action. Applying green maintenance principles and practices within your organizations is a step toward contributing to a more sustainable future.

Every energy efficiency choice, every waste management decision, and every conscious water use policy counts. You, as individuals and as part of larger collectives, have the power to influence and create change.

It is essential to recognize that the journey toward sustainability is one of continuous improvement. There is no "finish line" in sustainability; rather, it is a constant process of learning, adapting and growing.

The challenges will be inevitable, but the rewards - a healthier planet, resources preserved for future generations, and stronger, more resilient communities - are immeasurable.

In applying what you have learned in this book, I urge you to adopt a holistic and strategic approach.

Involve all stakeholders, from top management to operators, of the organization or company in its sustainability efforts.

Cultivate a culture of transparency, where goals, progress and challenges are communicated openly and honestly. And perhaps most importantly, be champions of change, demonstrating by example, the value and viability of green maintenance practices.

Ultimately, green maintenance is more than a series of technical tasks; it is a philosophy, a way of operating, that recognizes our interconnectedness with the natural world and our role in protecting it, the planet earth.

By embracing this philosophy, we not only protect the environment, but also ensure a more prosperous and sustainable future for our organization and the world at large.

This book is a call to action. It is in our hands, equipped with the necessary knowledge and tools, to make a difference. Together, we can transform maintenance from an operational necessity into a powerful force for good, ensuring that our impact on the planet is one of care, conservation and respect.

May this book be both a beacon and a map: lighting the way to more sustainable practices and guiding you through the complex but rewarding terrain of green maintenance. The journey to a greener, more sustainable future begins with small, determined steps toward change. It is up to us to take those steps and make a difference.

CONCLUSIONS

Ecological Imperative: Green maintenance has emerged as a critical need in the face of today's environmental challenges, proving to be not only a strategy for resource conservation, but also an imperative for the survival of ecosystems and society.

Multidimensional Benefits: Beyond its positive environmental impact, green maintenance offers significant economic benefits by reducing operating costs and improving efficiency, as well as contributing positively to corporate perception and reputation.

Cultural Transformation: Successful adoption of green maintenance requires a cultural transformation within organizations, where sustainability is integrated into the core of decision making and operational practices.

Innovation and Technology: The effective implementation of green maintenance relies on technological innovation, including the use of sensors, energy management systems and other digital tools that enable accurate monitoring and optimization of resources.

Education and Training: Ongoing training and education in sustainability, is critical to empower employees and ensure they understand their role, in implementing green maintenance practices.

Sectoral Collaboration: The case studies highlight the importance of collaboration between different sectors and industries to share knowledge, experiences and best practices in green maintenance, fostering a culture of continuous improvement.

Regulations and Certifications: The evolution of regulations and the development of green certifications, play a crucial role in setting standards for green maintenance, promoting the adoption of sustainable practices through incentives and recognition.

Implementation Challenges: Common challenges in implementing green maintenance, such as initial investment, resistance to change, and the need for strategic planning, can be overcome through effective change management and commitment from all levels of the organization.

Positive Social Impact: Green maintenance contributes significantly to social well-being by improving air quality, reducing pollution and creating healthier working and living environments for communities.

Sustainable Future: Finally, the book emphasizes that green maintenance is not just a trend, but a necessary evolution towards more responsible and sustainable operations, ensuring a more prosperous and equitable future for generations to come.

These appendices provide readers with a solid foundation of resources, a glossary for quick reference and a summary of standards, which are crucial to the understanding and application of green maintenance. Providing these additional resources facilitates continued learning and deeper understanding of sustainable practices.

APPENDIX A: ADDITIONAL RESOURCES

ADDITIONAL BOOKS AND PUBLICATIONS

"Sustainable Facility Management: The Facility Manager's Guide to Optimizing Building Performance" - John D. Wagner

A comprehensive manual on how facility managers can implement sustainable practices to improve building performance.

"The Green Workplace: Sustainable Strategies that Benefit Employees, the Environment, and the Bottom Line" - Leigh Stringer.

Explore strategies to create greener workplaces that benefit both employees and the environment.

"Green Maintenance for Buildings and Landscaping: An Administrator's Guide" - Sam Kubba

This book offers a comprehensive perspective on how to manage and maintain buildings and landscapes in a sustainable manner, addressing everything from energy efficiency to water and waste management.

"Eco-Friendly Building Materials and Construction Techniques" - Laura A. Wadhwa

An exploration of construction materials and techniques that minimize environmental impact, this book is essential for professionals interested in incorporating sustainability into infrastructure construction and maintenance.

ADDITIONAL ORGANIZATIONS AND WEBSITES

World Green Building Council (WorldGBC)

www.worldgbc.org

A global network of national green building councils, encouraging the adoption of sustainable construction and maintenance practices through collaborative projects, research and advocacy.

International Facility Management Association (IFMA)

www.ifma.org

It offers resources and training programs, focused on sustainable facilities management, with a wide range of educational materials on green maintenance.

Building Owners and Managers Association (BOMA) International

www.boma.org

Provides resources, standards and guidelines, on commercial property management with a focus on sustainability.

U.S. Green Building Council (USGBC)

www.usgbc.org

Provides extensive information on LEED certification and resources for sustainable construction and maintenance.

COURSES AND CERTIFICATIONS

LEED Green Associate Certification

A starting point for professionals seeking to demonstrate their knowledge of green building principles and sustainability.

Sustainability Management Course

Offered by various educational institutions and online platforms, these courses address topics ranging from environmental management to corporate sustainability.

Diploma in Green Maintenance Technologies

An intensive program covering advanced technologies in sustainable maintenance, from energy management to intelligent automation solutions.

Corporate Sustainability Certification

Focusing on how companies can integrate sustainable practices into their operations, this course addresses everything from corporate social responsibility to green maintenance strategies.

APPENDIX B: GLOSSARY OF KEY TERMS

Energy audit: Assessment carried out to measure the energy consumption of a facility or company and propose measures to improve energy efficiency and reduce consumption.

LEED (Leadership in Energy and Environmental Design) Certification: Certification system for buildings that meet criteria for energy efficiency, efficient use of water, reduction of CO_2 emissions, improvement of indoor environmental quality and resource management and sensitivity to their impacts.

Sustainable waste management: Practices involving the reduction, reuse and recycling of waste to minimize environmental impact.

ISO 14001: International standard, which specifies the requirements for an effective environmental management system that an organization can use to improve its environmental performance.

Waste minimization: Process of reducing the amount of waste generated by industrial processes and commercial activities through efficient practices.

Carbon neutrality: Achievement of a net zero carbon emissions balance through a combination of direct emission reductions and offsetting the remaining emissions through methods such as reforestation or carbon sequestration technologies.

Cleaner production: Continuous application of a preventive environmental strategy in processes, products and services to increase efficiency and reduce risks to humans and the environment.

Extended Producer Responsibility (EPR): Environmental policy, in which the producer is responsible for the entire life cycle of a product, especially in terms of collection, recycling and final disposal.

Industrial symbiosis: Sharing resources in a network of nearby companies and industries, such as materials, energy, water and/or by-products, to improve environmental efficiency.

Environmental management system (EMS): Part of an organization's management system used to develop and implement its environmental policy and manage its environmental aspects.

Electric vehicle (EV): Vehicles that use one or more electric motors for propulsion, reducing dependence on fossil fuels and reducing polluting emissions.

Zero Waste: Philosophy that promotes the reuse of all resources, through circular designs of products, processes and systems, to prevent waste disposal.

Biodiversity: The variety of life on the planet, including the diversity of species, ecosystems, and genetic differences within species. Biodiversity conservation is crucial for maintaining natural systems and ecosystem services.

Circular Economy: An economic model that seeks to minimize waste and maximize the use of resources. In the context of green maintenance, it involves the efficient use of resources and the maximization of the life cycle of materials and products.

Sustainability: Ability to meet present needs without compromising the ability of future generations to meet their own needs.

Energy Efficiency: Energy efficiency refers to the practice of reducing the amount of energy required to provide products and services. By improving energy efficiency, businesses, governments and consumers can achieve more while using fewer energy resources. This not only has economic benefits, such as reduced costs, but also significant environmental benefits, such as reduced emissions of greenhouse gases and other pollutants.

Climate Resilience: The ability to adapt to and survive the adverse effects of climate change. Green maintenance practices can improve the resilience of infrastructure and communities to extreme weather events.

Composting: The process of decomposing organic matter (such as food scraps and yard waste) into compost, a nutrient-rich fertilizer.

Ground cover: A layer of plants that covers the soil, used to protect it from erosion and improve its health. May include turf, native plants or cover crops.

Renewable energy: Energy generated from natural sources that are constantly replenished, such as the sun or wind, used in maintenance technologies to reduce dependence on fossil fuels.

Integrated Pest Management (IPM): Pest control strategy that combines biological, cultural, physical and chemical methods to minimize the use of pesticides and their environmental impact.

Carbon footprint: A measure of the environmental impact of certain actions in terms of the amount of greenhouse gases produced, measured in units of carbon dioxide.

Green infrastructure: Network of natural and semi-natural spaces with vegetation and bodies of water, which can provide ecological services and increase the quality of urban life.

Sustainable gardening: Gardening practices that reduce environmental impact, such as efficient water use, native plant selection and organic soil management.

Stormwater management: Techniques that capture, store and

treat rainwater to prevent pollution and overflow of drainage systems.

Permaculture: A system of agricultural and social principles that simulates the patterns and characteristics observed in natural ecosystems.

Recycling: The process of converting waste into usable materials to reduce the consumption of fresh resources and the accumulation of garbage.

Healthy soil: Soil that maintains a healthy ecological balance and supports plant and animal life, essential for green maintenance.

Xeriscaping: Landscape design that reduces or eliminates the need for additional irrigation through the use of drought-tolerant plants and efficient water management techniques.

Stakeholders: Refers to all those individuals, groups or entities that have an interest in or are affected by an organization's activities and decisions. Stakeholders can include a wide range of participants, such as employees, customers, suppliers, investors, local communities and government. Each of these groups can influence or be influenced by the success, policies, and actions of the company.

Internet of Things Application (IoTA) : The concept of Internet of Things Application (IoTA), refers to specific applications that use and manage Internet-connected devices, within the framework of the Internet of Things (IoT). The IoT is a network of physical objects - "things" - that are embedded with sensors, software and other technologies, for the purpose of connecting and exchanging data with other devices and systems via the Internet.

Artificial Intelligence (AI) : Refers to the simulation of human intelligence processes by computational systems. These processes include learning (acquiring information and rules for using the information), reasoning (using rules to reach approximate or definitive conclusions), and self-correction.

LED lighting: LED (light emitting diode) lighting is a highly efficient lighting technology that uses semiconductor diodes to convert electricity into light. Unlike traditional incandescent bulbs, which produce light by heating a filament until it glows, LEDs generate light when electrons flow through a semiconductor material and release energy, in the form of photons, a process known as electroluminescence.

Geographic Information Systems (GIS) are systems designed to capture, store, manipulate, analyze, manage and present all types of spatial or geographic data. This technology integrates hardware, software and data to manage and analyze data that is tied to a geographic location, allowing users to observe patterns, relationships and trends through visual maps, reports and graphs.

Heating, Ventilation, and Air Conditioning: HVAC stands for "Heating, Ventilation, and Air Conditioning". This term refers to the different systems used to move air between indoor and outdoor spaces, as well as to heat and cool residential, commercial and industrial buildings. HVAC systems are essential to ensure a comfortable indoor environment by maintaining the right air quality and temperature.

Energy Management Systems (EMS): These are structured frameworks or systems used by organizations to monitor, control and optimize energy use in their operations. The main objective of an EMS is to improve energy efficiency, thus reducing total energy consumption, associated costs and environmental impact.

Water Management: Strategies and practices designed to optimize water use, including conservation, reuse and treatment.

Key Performance Indicators (KPIs): Key Performance Indicators are quantifiable metrics used to evaluate the success of an organization, employee, project or activity in meeting previously defined objectives. These indicators are essential for companies and organizations, as they provide a clear and objective way to measure performance and operational efficiency, as well as being a crucial tool for decision making and strategic planning.

Intelligent Building Management Systems (BMS): (Building

Management Systems) are advanced systems that centralize and control the infrastructure and services of a building, to optimize its operation, increase its efficiency and improve the comfort of the occupants. These systems integrate various building functions, such as HVAC, lighting, energy, water consumption, security and other operational systems, through a centralized interface.

REACH (Registration, Evaluation, Authorization and Restriction of Chemicals) Regulation of the European Union, which was established to improve the protection of human health and the environment from the risks that chemicals may present. REACH also promotes alternative methods for risk assessment of substances to reduce animal testing.

Carbon Footprint: A term commonly used to describe the total amount of carbon dioxide (CO_2) and other greenhouse gas (GHG) emissions that are emitted directly or indirectly by human activities or specific products throughout their life cycle. However, "Carbon Footprint" can also refer to tools or platforms, which allow individuals, companies and organizations to calculate and manage their carbon footprint.

The Global Reporting Initiative (GRI) is an independent international organization that has developed one of the most widely used frameworks for sustainability reporting by companies and organizations. Founded in 1997, GRI promotes the use of sustainability reporting as a way for organizations to be more transparent about their impacts on the economy, environment and society. GRI's mission is to help companies, governments and other organizations understand and communicate these impacts, both positive and negative, with the goal of fostering better global sustainability.

APPENDIX C: SUMMARY OF RELEVANT STANDARDS

ISO 55000:2014 - ASSET MANAGEMENT SYSTEM

ISO 55000 refers to a set of international standards dedicated to asset management. Developed and published by the International Organization for Standardization (ISO), this family of standards provides a framework for the systematic management of an organization's physical assets throughout their life cycle. Its main objective is to help organizations manage their assets effectively and efficiently, ensuring that maximum value is obtained from them while minimizing associated costs and risks.

COMPONENTS OF THE ISO 55000 STANDARD

The ISO 55000 series consists of several parts, including:

ISO 55000: Provides an overview of asset management principles and terminology. This document establishes the context, terms and definitions related to asset management, serving as a starting point for understanding the overall approach of the series.

ISO 55001: Specifies the requirements for an asset management system. This part of the standard details the specific requirements that an organization needs to meet to establish, implement, maintain and improve an asset management system. It covers aspects such as asset management policy, planning, implementation, performance evaluation and continual improvement.

ISO 55002: Provides guidelines for the implementation of an asset management system in accordance with ISO 55001. It provides additional guidance and examples of how to apply the requirements of ISO 55001, making it easier for organizations to interpret and effectively implement an asset management system.

BENEFITS OF ISO 55000 IMPLEMENTATION

Asset management optimization: Helps organizations improve decision making related to the acquisition, use and disposal of assets.

Improved performance and sustainability: Promotes practices that increase efficiency and sustainability in asset management, contributing to cost reduction and increased profitability.

Risk reduction: Enables organizations to identify, analyze and manage risks associated with assets, which can lead to increased security and reduced losses.

Regulatory compliance: Supports organizations in complying with legal, regulatory and other requirements related to their assets.

Improved reputation: By adopting an internationally recognized framework for asset management, organizations can improve their image with stakeholders, including investors, customers and the general public.

APPLICABILITY

The ISO 55000 series is applicable to any type of organization, regardless of its size, type or the assets it owns. It is relevant to sectors that rely heavily on physical assets for their operation, such as manufacturing, energy, transportation and public infrastructure, but can also be useful for organizations in other sectors seeking to improve the efficiency and value obtained from their assets.

ISO 14001 - ENVIRONMENTAL MANAGEMENT

ISO 14001: This standard provides a framework for an effective environmental management system (EMS). It enables organizations to improve their environmental performance through a more efficient use of resources and a reduction of waste, in line with the principles of green maintenance.

ISO 50001 - ENERGY MANAGEMENT

ISO 50001: Focused on improving energy efficiency, this standard helps organizations to establish the systems and processes needed to improve their energy performance. This includes the efficient use of energy during the maintenance of equipment and facilities, which is a central aspect of green maintenance.

ISO 14040 AND 14044 - LIFE CYCLE ANALYSIS (LCA)

ISO 14040 and ISO 14044: These standards provide the framework and guidelines for carrying out life cycle analysis, respectively. LCA assesses the environmental impacts associated with all stages of a product or service's life, from the extraction of raw materials to its final disposal. LCA can help identify opportunities to improve maintenance practices from an environmental perspective.

ISO 14064 - GREENHOUSE GASES

ISO 14064: This series of standards provides tools for quantifying and managing greenhouse gas emissions. This can be relevant to green maintenance in terms of monitoring and reducing emissions associated with the maintenance of buildings and infrastructure.

ISO 14020 - ENVIRONMENTAL LABELS AND DECLARATIONS

ISO 14020, ISO 14021, ISO 14024, and ISO 14025: These standards provide principles and guidelines for all types of environmental labels and declarations, including self-declarations, eco-labels and environmental product declarations. The use of products and services that comply with these guidelines can be a component of green maintenance, ensuring that the materials and procedures used are environmentally preferable.

GREEN SEAL

A certification program that evaluates products and services for their environmental impact, promoting more sustainable alternatives for the maintenance and operation of buildings.

These additional and expanded resources offer green maintenance professionals, academics and enthusiasts a rich and diverse compendium of tools and knowledge.

By leveraging these resources, stakeholders can drive the adoption of sustainable maintenance practices, contributing significantly to overall conservation and sustainability efforts.

DIRECTORY OF GREEN TECHNOLOGY SUPPLIERS AND MANUFACTURERS

(Fictitious, the author does not intend to divert attention to specific companies, but rather that the interested parties, individuals or companies investigate the broad world market and define their priorities in this field).

This fictitious directory serves as a starting point to identify and connect with potential green technology suppliers and manufacturers.

When selecting business partners, it is essential to consider not only the range of products and services offered, but also the company's commitment to sustainable practices and its track record in implementing effective green maintenance solutions.

RENEWABLE ENERGY

SolarTech Innovations

Description: Leading manufacturer of solar panels and solar energy solutions for residential and commercial use.

Location: San Francisco, California, United States.

Web site: www.solartechinnovations.com

Featured Products/Services: Solar panels, mounting systems, solar inverters.

WindPower Solutions

Description: Global supplier of wind turbines and installation and maintenance services for wind farms.

Location: Hamburg, Germany

Web site: www.windpowersolutions.com

Featured Products/Services: Wind turbines, wind project consulting, turbine maintenance.

WATER AND WASTE MANAGEMENT

AquaPurify

Description: Specialists in water treatment technologies and recycling solutions for industries and municipalities.

Location: Amsterdam, The Netherlands

Web site: www.aquapurify.nl

Featured Products/Services: Water filtration systems, wastewater treatment plants, water management consulting services.

EcoWaste Solutions

Description: Innovator in waste management solutions, offering products and services to minimize the environmental impact of waste.

Location: Toronto, Canada

Web site: www.ecowastesolutions.ca

Featured Products/Services: Composting systems, recycling technologies, waste management consulting.

ENERGY EFFICIENCY

GreenBuild Products

Description: Manufacturer of sustainable building materials and energy efficient solutions for buildings.

Location: London, United Kingdom

Web site: www.greenbuildproducts.co.uk

Product/Service Highlights: Ecological insulation, double-glazed windows, energy-saving LED lighting systems.

Efficient HVAC Solutions

Description: Supplier of high efficiency heating, ventilation and air conditioning (HVAC) systems for residential and commercial applications.

Location: Sydney, Australia

Web site: www.efficienthvac.com.au

Featured Products/Services: Heat pumps, efficient HVAC systems, installation and maintenance services.

ABOUT THE AUTHOR

Engineer Gilberth Bolaños F. emerges as a pioneer in the transformation of industrial maintenance towards sustainable and environmentally conscious practices.

A graduate in electromechanical engineering from the prestigious Instituto Tecnológico, his more than two decades of experience in the field of business maintenance and environmental management have established him as an undisputed authority on sustainable development.

With a revolutionary vision, Mr. Bolaños has led the way in reforming traditional maintenance, adapting it to the imperatives of our era.

Its approach not only seeks to optimize operational efficiency, but also to incorporate strategies that reduce environmental impact and promote sustainability at the heart of industrial operations.

This vision, rooted in innovation and sustainability, has set a new direction for responsible and effective business practices.

Through this book, Mr. Bolaños F. generously shares his vast knowledge and experience, providing companies and government agencies with the necessary tools to adopt maintenance that not only responds to current demands, but also anticipates future challenges.

His work is presented as an indispensable resource for

those committed to the conservation of the planet, offering fresh perspectives and pragmatic solutions to overcome environmental challenges through renewed and sustainable industrial maintenance.

Recognized and respected by colleagues and industry leaders, Bolaños F. has been a fervent promoter of change, inspiring countless professionals to re-evaluate and adapt their maintenance methods in favor of greener and more sustainable practices.

His legacy, embodied in the pages of this book, is an invitation to be part of a movement that goes beyond mere regulatory compliance to embrace an ethic of care and respect for our planet.

In this book, Engineer Gilberth Bolaños F., not only teaches us how green maintenance can be effectively implemented, but also how it can serve as a cornerstone for a more prosperous and sustainable future.

With each chapter, he guides us on a path of discovery, challenging us to rethink our current practices and take concrete steps toward a deeper commitment to the sustainability of life on planet Earth.

www.ingramcontent.com/pod-product-compliance
Lightning Source LLC
Chambersburg PA
CBHW050102230526
45470CB00004B/1641